1936-1945 LIFE
The First Decade

D0523182

Cover

Bourke-White, Margaret/1936
Construction of giant pipes which will be used
to divert a section of the Missouri River during
the building of the Fort Peck Dam.
10 x 13¼ inches

Library of Congress Catalog Card Number 79-88091
International Standard Book Number: 0-8212-0760-1

New York Graphic Society books are published by
Little, Brown and Company. Published simultaneously
in Canada by Little, Brown and Company (Canada)
Limited.

LIFE
1936-1945
The First Decade

New York Graphic Society
Boston

Introduction
Robert R. Littman,
Director Grey Art Gallery & Study Center

This exhibition is a representative selection and a comprehensive view of LIFE Magazine's achievement during its first decade of publication.

More than one hundred thousand vintage prints were available from that decade, and this number was first reduced to twenty thousand. The formidable and discerning task of selecting from this group the final two hundred photographs had its delights and satisfactions as well as its compromises and wrenching decisions. The hardest decisions came when we were paring down the last five hundred, for these were the most difficult to say good-bye to. I persist in thinking that there may be an equally compelling exhibition in the piles of pictures we were forced to leave out.

There are images here so closely associated with the period or with a specific event that they have come to symbolize a particular moment. Presenting the image recalls that moment in the full spectrum of its original emotion. Such images were obvious first choices. But we have tried to steer away from the overly exposed, the impending cliche. Because of the nature of LIFE Magazine, we were able to divide our picture groups into human behavior, inanimate objects and events. The biggest single group of photographs in the exhibition shows the trauma and triumph of World War II.

In some cases captions ascribe a picture to a Time Inc. publication other than LIFE. This is because once the photographs had been taken, they were filed in the Picture Collection and could then be used by any of the Time Inc. magazines. What originally had been assigned to a LIFE staff photographer might later be retrieved and matched to a story appearing in FORTUNE or TIME.

We have not been able to include here any complete LIFE picture stories, which often ran to twenty or thirty published pictures on a single subject. There is certainly another specialized exhibition in this category of work that was so closely associated with and perfected by LIFE.

In fact, from these archives many diverse exhibitions could be organized. Our objective in this first exhibition was to present the spectrum of possibilities within a comprehensive format, concentrating on the first decade of a publication that affected the way America perceived itself and the world. LIFE had a decided editorial policy, perhaps unconscious, perhaps naive. It favored the inherent good in man; a positive future, apple pie and "the American way of life"; the dignity in hardship, the eventual triumph over adversity; the forces of nature and the destiny of America. And it said all this in pictures.

Perhaps LIFE's own perspective became a self-fulfilling prophecy during these years. The magazine certainly found a large audience in all the economic and social and racial strata of our society. LIFE was good, it was good value, it was a quality publication that esteemed the photograph.

This exhibition reviews those years as reflected in the lenses of LIFE's photographers. We hope we have done justice to such a distinguished body of work.

Note: This introduction was written for an exhibition of these photographs which opened at the Grey Art Gallery in 1979.

A search for reality created works of art
Ralph Graves
Corporate Editor, Time Inc.

The 200 vintage prints in this book come from LIFE's first decade—the years 1936-45. The great majority of them were published in the magazine. I think you will agree that they are not only a remarkable journalistic record and reminder of those years but are also works of art. That is why the Grey Gallery of New York University chose to mount and present the exhibition.

However, few of these pictures were intended to be works of art. Most were shot by hardworking journalists who were trying to record the world around them in order to fill the pages of LIFE. The weekly magazine had an enormous appetite for good photographs. Since the editors were journalists, they wanted pictures that reported on the news, on people and events, on life itself. That is why there is so much realism in this book—and such evocation of the flavor and character of that time.

Each week LIFE sent out hundreds of prints to be engraved and published. When they were returned to the New York office, they might easily have been discarded, on the familiar theory that nothing is older than last week's news. Fortunately the editors decided they just might want to publish some of the pictures again some day, either in LIFE or in one of the company's other publications. So they were kept.

What began as a small batch of pictures with dubious value is today a huge, important and immensely useful collection—more than 18 million images, including prints, negatives and color transparencies. It is the largest privately owned collection in the world, and it is meticulously filed, captioned, indexed and cross-indexed. Our magazines draw from it constantly, both for pictures to publish and for pictures as a research tool, to reveal how things once looked or what people once did. The many books that we publish also rely heavily on the resources of the Collection. And not only do Time Inc. magazines and books use it on a daily basis, but so do many interested outside authors, scholars, publishers and businesses.

The excellence of the Collection—and indeed, its very survival—must be credited primarily to one person. Doris O'Neil first came to work in the Picture Collection 30 years ago and ran it for 22 years.

She loved pictures—an obvious criterion for that job—but she also thought they were historically and artistically important. She wanted to preserve as many of the original prints as possible, and so she was always conniving for floor space, filing cabinets, cataloguers and researchers.

Doris O'Neil called the LIFE Picture Collection "Fort Knox" and tried to persuade everyone in the company that it was an invaluable treasury. At the same time, she wanted the pictures to be in constant use and was always happy to get requests for them. She was less happy if the pictures were not returned promptly, and in good condition. Every print was logged out and logged in. An editor or art director who failed to return a set of pictures would get reminder notices and crisp phone calls. New LIFE reporters were given indoctrination talks about the use and abuse of pictures and the importance of writing proper caption information.

Doris O'Neil put some 800 exceptionally important prints in a separate "Famous Picture" file. You could borrow one of these original prints from the Collection if you convinced her that you had a serious need for it, although a bright orange sticker on the back commanded you to return the print to her personally. If she decided that your need for a "Famous Picture" was less than serious, she would make a copy print for you, but she would hang on to the original.

The result of all her years of strenuous promotion and equally strenuous protection is that the pictures are still in daily use and yet superbly preserved. Her work has made this book possible.

This selection of vintage prints from the first decade of LIFE was made by Doris O'Neil and by Robert Littman, the Director of the Grey Art Gallery. Many great photographic names are represented. From among the LIFE staff photographers (surely that was the most glamorous job in journalism) there are such names as Margaret Bourke-White, Alfred Eisenstaedt, Carl Mydans, W. Eugene Smith. Among those who were never on the staff but who took pictures for the magazine, are Edward Weston, Charles Sheeler, Cecil Beaton, Ansel Adams, Berenice Abbott and many others.

In view of the rich diversity of this selection, it is interesting to realize that these pictures make up roughly 1/90,000 of the LIFE Picture Collection. It is therefore a very tiny tip of the iceberg, but I hope you will agree that it is an exceptional tip.

LIFE's Picture Collection
Doris C. O'Neil,
Director of Vintage Prints, Time Inc.

In the excitement of LIFE's immediate success, no one had the time or inclination to think about a problem that began to develop a few months after the first issue...how to organize the mountain of photographs that was rapidly piling up in the editorial offices. Photographers all over the world, LIFE's own staff photographers and the commercial photo agencies as well, were hourly adding to this mountain. Since its size doubled with predictable regularity, a staff of two was eventually hired to face the problem. No immediate sources were available in print or elsewhere to tell them how to plan and operate a picture collection on that scale which was capable of functioning at the speed LIFE's editors required. There was nothing for the staff to do but plunge in and try. Eventually the beginnings of a system began to emerge from the chaos.

The major, pioneer work of developing those beginnings, of devising a classification system and of applying a pattern of organization was done by Margaret Gallagher and Grace Young, who were the department's original staff of two and who worked at its problems for over 30 years. Many other persons have played important roles in the development of the Picture Collection but these are the ones who laid the foundation upon which it still rests.

Gallagher, as she insisted on being called, had come to LIFE from direct-mail promotion at the recently defunct Delineator Magazine. Grace joined the department from a career at what was then known as the Chase National Bank. As they labored at their task, they probably had no thought in their heads of establishing what has since become the largest indexed collection of photographs in the world. Undoubtedly their strongest motivation was one of survival and an understandable dislike of the looming prospect of being buried alive under nearly 10 tons of photographic paper.

Meanwhile, in my home state of Rhode Island, I too was beginning work with picture collections but on a very much smaller scale. The collecting of pictures has had a fascination for me all my life. I clearly remember the moment I first became conscious of this fascination. Our second-grade teacher, a Miss Clarke, after showing us some seasonal pictures that she admired, remarked that throughout the year she collected pictures she liked and kept them in order so when she wanted them she could find them. That simple sentence had such a profound effect on me that I can remember even the dress I was wearing at the time; it was a black and yellow plaid. I don't know whether that comment touched some hidden spring in me that was just waiting to burst forth or whether it in effect programmed me to a course of action. At any rate from then on I knew the kind of work I wanted to do.

Soon after this I began my own collection of pictures and this developing interest eventually led me to the picture collections of the Providence Public Library and the Rhode Island School of Design. I realized later that I began my apprenticeship in the Public Library's picture collection at just about the same time Gallagher and Grace were beginning their labors at LIFE.

While my interest was in the whole field of graphics and illustration my experience at the School of Design focused this interest on photography. I also became aware that increasingly my interest was in the display of photographs as the best way of sharing with others the gems I discovered. I was, of course, fascinated by LIFE Magazine and when I realized LIFE had an exhibition department… one of their exhibitions came to the School of Design…I thought how wonderful it would be to work there. I went to LIFE to explore this possibility only to learn that department was soon to come to an end. It was suggested that there might be an opening for me in the Picture Collection. That thought pleased me almost as much as working with exhibitions, and when a job was offered to me, I accepted immediately.

I remember once having said to friends that my idea of happiness would be to be in a room with a million pictures. When I arrived at LIFE's Picture Collection in 1948 it contained over 2 million photographs and I was very happy.

I realized at an early stage that collecting pictures is easy. But keeping them in order so that they can be found when they are wanted (in the words of that second-grade teacher) is not so easy. In a collection the size of LIFE's, it is very difficult. It was with a sense of dedication that I added my efforts to those of Grace and Gallagher and their associates to develop and improve the system they had established.

Another problem which became apparent when the Collection was 12 or 15 years old was the problem of space. Increasingly this dominated all discussions about the Picture Collection for the next 25 years. The Collection's rate of growth made it inevitable that it would eventually have space problems. Miniaturization, beyond a certain point, was not the answer since editors and art directors insisted upon seeing full-size prints to judge photographic quality.

The problem was aggravated by the economic pressures in the late '50s, and again in the early '70s. The Picture Collection occupies the west end of the 28th floor of the Time-Life Building which, in a north and south direction, is a city block deep. This is very expensive real estate and business managers and other planners during those 20 years constantly explored ways to move us from it. We, for our part, applied every method we could think of to control our size. We shifted from 3-drawer file cabinets to 4-drawer cabinets. We put file cabinets where aisles had been and the few aisles we kept, we made very narrow. Nevertheless, our floor space was reduced until in 1970 we were a third smaller than we had been 10 years earlier. We could not compress any further and we reached the point where a stand had to be taken. A great deal of psychological warfare was waged back and forth during those years but we outlived, one by one, each of the dozen or so plans to give us away or pack us off to the Jersey meadows.

The Picture Collection has survived to become a source file of vast richness and a research tool of incalculable value, outstanding not only because of its size but more importantly because of the quality of its contents. Its organization has been studied for its ideas and patterns by foreign governments, national museums, universities, publishers and the Armed Forces. It contains images on every subject under the sun or the far side of the moon and new photographs are added at the average rate of nearly 1,000 a week. In terms of time its scope ranges from the oldest fossils known to man to subjects which cannot be seen by the human eye and respond only to special newly developed techniques. Two-thirds of the photographs in the Collection are of people, reflecting LIFE's preoccupation with people. Alphabetically the range is from Aa, Pieter, a 17th century German etcher, to Zyromski, Jean, a 20th century government figure.

Work in the Collection can be demanding and exacting and sometimes frustrating and discouraging. But I firmly believe that it is the best place in all of Time Incorporated to enjoy photography. The photographs in this book are only a small fraction of the thousands I have enjoyed during all these years. Some of them have not been published before…the small boy with the Fourth of July hat and the faraway thoughts; the group with endearing sincerity pledging allegiance to the flag; the young girl studying her image in the mirrored section of a garden wall. Most of the photographs here are being seen for the first time since they appeared in LIFE 30 or 40 years ago. It is my hope that many, many persons seeing these photographs will find them to be the enduring source of pleasure they have been for me.

1936-1945

LIFE
The First Decade

Bourke-White, Margaret/1936
Construction workers and taxi-dancers shuffle
away a Saturday night in a frontier barroom.
This photograph was the lead picture in
LIFE's first story, a picture essay on the
construction of a major dam at Fort Peck,
Montana.
LIFE November 23, 1936
10¼ x 13½ inches

Stern, Phil/1945
Unemployed shipyard worker heads home to
Tennessee at the close of World War II.
LIFE September 3, 1945
7⅝ x 9⅛ inches

Eisenstaedt, Alfred/1943
Father and son, owners of a 35,000 acre
ranch in west Texas.
13⅛ x 10⅝ inches   Signed on back.

Rothstein, Arthur/1936
Father and sons in a dust storm, Cimarron
County, Oklahoma.
LIFE February 26, 1940
7½ x 7⅝ inches

Eisenstaedt, Alfred/1942
From an essay on the state of Oklahoma.
7½ x 9⅝ inches   Signed on back.

Eisenstaedt, Alfred/1937
Widow is escorted from the cemetery after the
burial of her husband.
8 x 10 inches   Signed on back.

Bristol, Horace/1938
This, and the photograph on page 11, were
among those taken by Bristol when he and
John Steinbeck toured California's migratory
labor camps, in search of a story for LIFE and
material for a picture book. The idea of a
picture book was dropped but from this
assignment grew the idea for Steinbeck's
most famous book, "The Grapes of Wrath."
The woman shown here was the inspiration
for Ma Joad.
LIFE June 5, 1939
9⅜ x 7½ inches

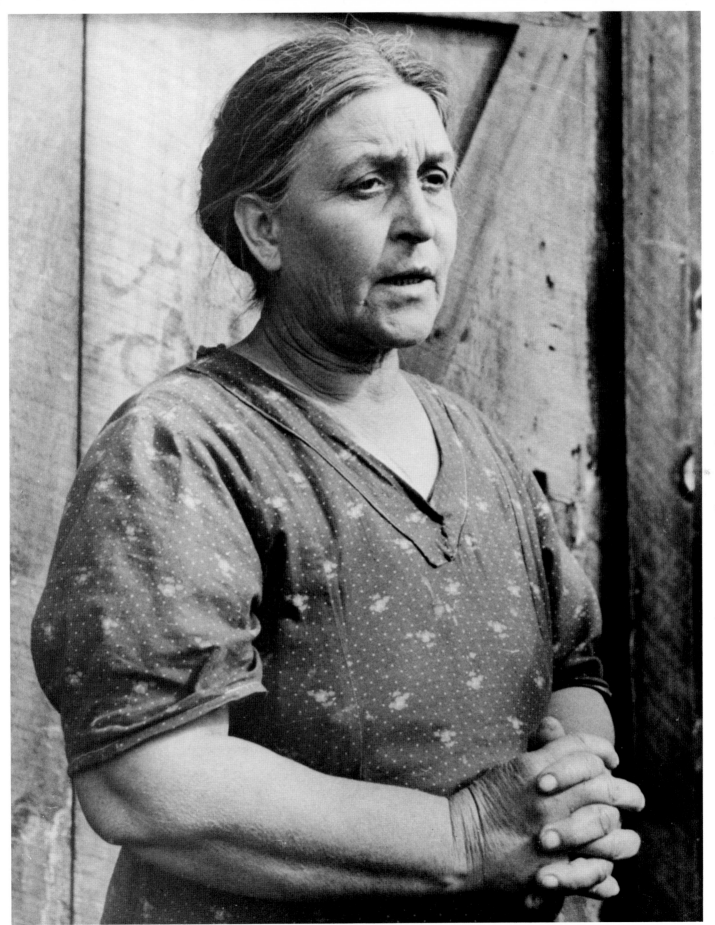

Mydans, Carl/1938
Barmaid in the oil boom town of Freer, Texas.
LIFE January 17, 1938
10 x 13¼ inches   Signed on back.

Bristol, Horace/1938
The struggle to find work. See caption for
photograph on page 8.
LIFE June 5, 1939
9 x 7½ inches

Bristol, Horace/1939
American frontier, 1939. An Idaho farm on the
Salmon River at the base of the Pahsimeroi
Mountains.
LIFE June 5, 1939
10¼ x 13¼ inches

Adams, Ansel/1944
March sun and wind start to break up the ice
on the lakes in the California mountains.
LIFE April 24, 1944
10⅛ x 13 inches

Coster, Gordon/1943
Harvest near East Grand Forks, Minnesota.
Workers pause briefly for lunch brought to the
fields by women of their families.
LIFE September 27, 1943
10⅝ x 13⅜ inches

Vandivert, William/1938
William Lyon Phelps at the gate of his summer
home in Michigan.
LIFE December 5, 1938
9⅞ x 13¼ inches

Smith, W. Eugene/1940
Flag Day in South Bend, Indiana. Pledging
allegiance to the flag.
13⅜ x 10½ inches.

Gehr, Herbert/1942
Raymond L. Buell running for the Republican
nomination for a Massachusetts
Congressional seat.
LIFE August 24, 1942
13 x 10¼ inches

Eisenstaedt, Alfred/1942
With sons home from the National Guard for
the weekend, a Kansas family spends
Sunday afternoon on its front porch in
Emporia.
LIFE November 9, 1942
13⅜ x 10½ inches.   Signed on back.

Bourke-White, Margaret/1939
Small boy observes the Fourth of July,
Woodhaven Hall, Watervliet, N.Y. From the
Hudson River essay.
13¼ x 9⅞ inches

Eisenstaedt, Alfred/1942
Daughter of an Oklahoma farmer reads in her
room, preparing for high school in the fall.
LIFE July 13, 1942
13¼ x 10½ inches   Signed on back.

Mydans, Carl/1939
Worker calls out measurements to co-workers
forging a tunnel under New York's East River.
LIFE September 21, 1959
12¾ x 10⅛ inches   Signed on back.

Bourke-White, Margaret/1939
Hooded worker sandblasts airplane cylinder
heads. From Aluminum Company of America
essay.
13⅜ x 10 inches.

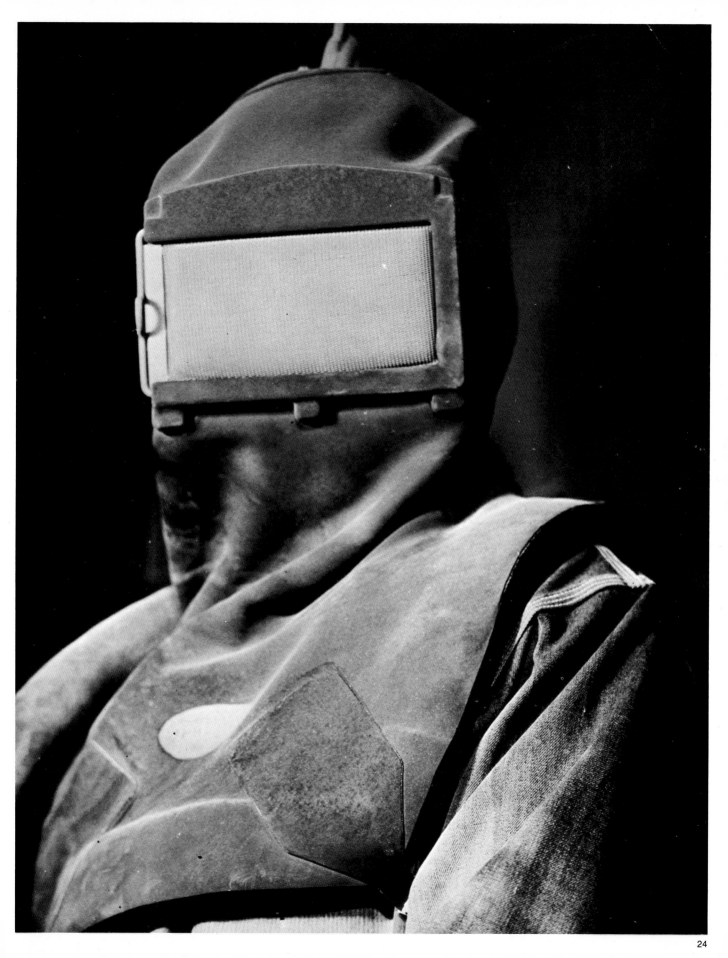

Lofman, Jacob/1944
John Dow Farrington, chief of the Rock Island
Railroad, travels over all parts of the railroad's
system in his private car, giving special
attention to track maintenance.
FORTUNE December 1944
12⅞ x 10⅜ inches

Stackpole, Peter/1942
Fireman in the cab of a switch engine in the
Roseville, California yard. From Southern
Pacific Railroad essay.
LIFE September 21, 1942
13⅛ x 10½ inches

Bourke-White, Margaret/1936
Construction of giant pipes which will be used
to divert a section of the Missouri River during
the building of the Fort Peck Dam.
10 x 13¼ inches

Feininger, Andreas/1944
Pouring steel from an open-hearth furnace at
the Carnegie-Illinois Steel Company plant,
Pittsburgh, Pennsylvania.
13⅜ x 10½ inches

Sheeler, Charles/1927
One of a series of 32 photographs which
Sheeler made during the six weeks he spent
at the Ford plant at Dearborn, Michigan.
LIFE August 8, 1938
9⅜ x 7½ inches   Signature, title and date on back.

Bourke-White, Margaret/1939
Worker tears off a sample from a roll of paper
to test its quality. Savannah, Georgia.
LIFE May 15, 1939
10 x 13¼ inches

Bourke-White, Margaret/1939
Coiled aluminum rods ready for drawing into wire.
10 x 13¼ inches

Bourke-White, Margaret/1938
Model for the 50-foot New York World's Fair
sundial by Paul Manship, representing the
Three Fates with the Thread of Life.
LIFE January 31, 1938
13¼ x 10 inches

Bourke-White, Margaret/1936
Gold being cooled after it had been melted
down to be reshaped into standard U.S.
bricks.
LIFE December 14, 1936
13½ x 10 inches

Sarra, Valentino/1936
Radiator detail of the 1937 Nash.
TIME November 16, 1936
10⅜ x 13 inches

Edgerton, Harold E./1939
Stroboscopic study of the impact on a
telephone book of a golf ball traveling at 225
feet per second.
LIFE November 20, 1939
7¾ x 9⅝ inches

Evans, Walker/1934
Newsstand displaying Communist
publications. From a story on the Communist
Party in the United States.
FORTUNE September 1934
6 x 8⅜ inches

Van Dyke, Willard/1938
Old Spanish church in New Mexico.
7⅝ x 9½ inches

Munkacsi, Martin/1939
Cowboy's Stetson on a corral post. From
essay on a dude ranch.
LIFE June 19, 1939
11⅜ x 9 inches

Beaton, Cecil/1940
Wilton House, home of Lord and Lady
Pembroke. The view from the library,
dismantled for the duration of World War II, is
of the garden where Sir Philip Sidney wrote
"Arcadia" in 1580.
9¾ x 9⅝ inches

Leen, Nina/1945
Santa Lucia mountain range between Carmel
and San Simeon, California. The old chair
was from an abandoned cabin on the site.
10⅞ x 12⅛ inches   Signed on back.

Weston, Edward/1936
One of a series of studies of sand dunes,
Oceano, California
LIFE April 12, 1937
7½ x 9½ inches

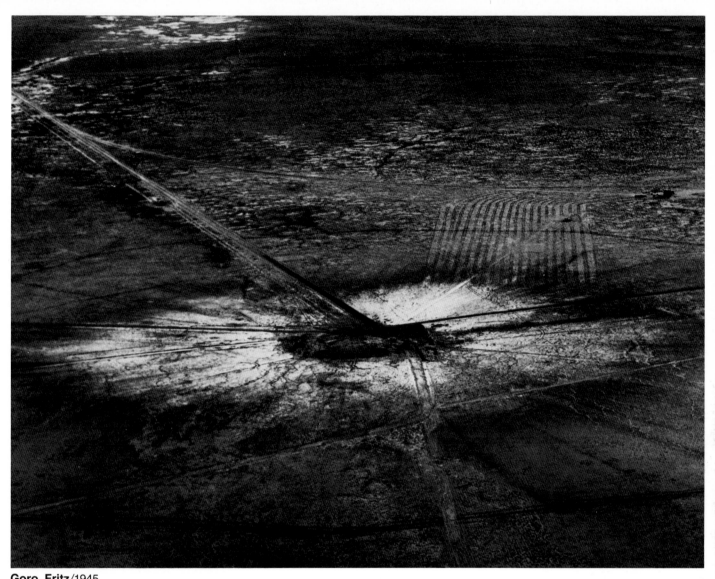

Goro, Fritz/1945
Bomb crater of the first atomic bomb in the
New Mexico desert near Alamogordo. The
lighter area around the dark center is a layer
of glass 2,400 feet across, formed from the
sand by the bomb's intense heat.
LIFE September 24, 1945
10½ x 13½ inches   Signed on back.

Manzon-Match/1939
Nijinsky responds as Serge Lifar, ballet
master of the Paris Opera, dances for him in
the Swiss sanatorium where Nijinsky had
been confined for 20 years following his
mental breakdown.
LIFE July 3, 1939
7 x 9½ inches

Manzon-Match/1939
Suddenly and unexpectedly Nijinsky leaps
into the air and the photographer manages to
catch this historic moment.
LIFE July 3, 1939
9½ × 7 inches

Brodsky, Michel/1937
Colette's feet, shod in her usual sandals.
LIFE December 20, 1937
9½ x 7⅛ inches

48

Stackpole, Peter/1942
Jean Renoir discusses a reproduction of a
painting by his father, Auguste Renoir, with his
father's famous model, Gabrielle.
10¼ x 12⅛ inches

Adams, Ansel/1938
Georgia O'Keeffe gathering material in New
Mexico for her paintings.
LIFE February 14, 1938
9⅛ x 7 inches   Signed on back.

Munkacsi, Martin/ca. 1938
Diego Rivera with his wife, Frieda Kahlo.
LIFE March 14, 1938
11½ x 9⅛ inches

Jackson, Ray Lee/1937
Gertrude Stein, photographed on her visit to
the United States in 1937.
LIFE August 27, 1945
6½ x 4 inches

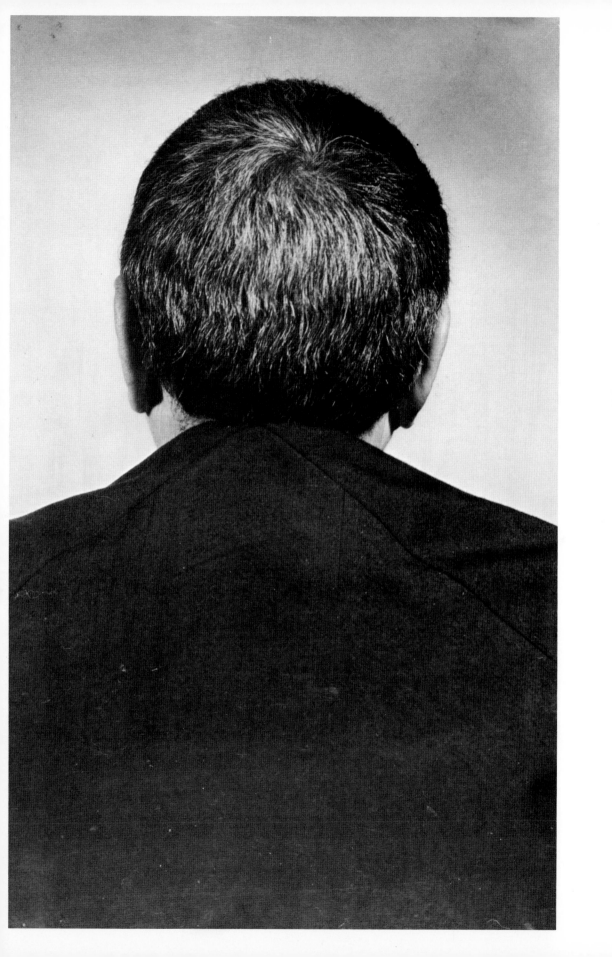

Eisenstaedt, Alfred/1939
One of a series of architectural studies of
the New York World's Fair taken before its
opening in April, 1939.
9⅝ x 7⅝ inches   Signed on back.

Scherman, David E./1939
On opening day, visitors to the New York
World's Fair walk from the Trylon into the
Perisphere.
LIFE May 15, 1939
11 x 10¼ inches

Kitrosser, I./1937
Entrance to the Optique, at the Paris
Exposition of 1937.
9½ x 7⅛ inches

Gehr, Herbert/1939
New building of the Museum of Modern Art,
designed by Philip L. Goodwin and Edward D.
Stone, opened on the occasion of the
Museum's 10th birthday in 1939.
13½ x 10½ inches

Korling, Torkel/1939
Carport of the Johnson Wax Company
Building in Racine, Wisconsin. Designed
by Frank Lloyd Wright, the building is of
cantilever construction. The domes joined
together help support the roof, reducing the
number of support columns needed.
LIFE May 8, 1939
12½ x 9⅞ inches

Korling, Torkel/1939
President Herbert Fisk Johnson, left, on the
balcony of Frank Lloyd Wright's Johnson Wax
Company buildings.
9⅞ x 12½ inches

Munkacsi, Martin/1936
Variety of steps in the Lindy Hop.
LIFE December 28, 1936
Each 5⅝ x 4⅜ inches

Stackpole, Peter/1937
Saturday night at Dartmouth's Winter
Carnival.
LIFE February 22, 1937
13⅛ x 10 inches

Smith, W. Eugene/1941
Congeroo, a combination of the Lindy Hop
and the Conga, as performed at the Savoy.
LIFE June 16, 1941
10⅛ x 13¼ inches

Mili, Gjon/1944
Repetitive strobe portrait of Gene Kelly.
10⅜ x 13¼ inches

Harris, Martin/1939
Uncle Wallace Howland, Cape Cod expert,
swings two young partners in "Fisherman's
Reel."
LIFE October 9, 1939
11½ x 9 inches

Munkacsi, Martin/1936
Fred Astaire in a dance routine.
LIFE December 28, 1936
11⅝ x 8¼ inches

Bourke-White, Margaret/1938
Parents of Konrad Henlein, Nazi leader of
the Sudeten Germans, in their home in
Czechoslovakia.
LIFE May 30, 1938
10 x 13¼ inches

Beaton, Cecil/1940
Lord Shrewsbury's secretary, Mr. Thompson,
watering Lord Shrewsbury's plants at Ingestre
Hall, Staffordshire.
9⅞ x 8⅝ inches

Eisenstaedt, Alfred/1937
Patient resting at Trudeau Sanatorium,
Saranac Lake, New York.
LIFE November 29, 1937
10⅛ x 7⅝ inches   Signed on back.

Eisenstaedt, Alfred/1932
Opera audience at La Scala, Milan.
LIFE September 4, 1944
13¾ x 10⅞ inches   Signed on back.

O'Reilly, Gray
Pope Pius XII, as Cardinal Pacelli, in the living
room of Mrs. Genevieve Brady, his hostess
during his 1936 tour of the United States.
LIFE March 13, 1939
10¾ x 15 inches

Prince, Erney from P.I.
Library in one of the colleges within the
Vatican.
14⅛ x 11 inches

Wilding, Dorothy/1939
Gertrude Lawrence and Douglas Fairbanks, Jr.
9½ x 10 inches

Munkacsi, Martin
Mae West.
11⅜ x 9⅛ inches

Cooke, Jerry/1944
Martha Graham executing a characteristic
turn.
13⅜ x 10⅝ inches

Landry, Bob/1945
Fred Astaire working out the fine points of his
dance, Putting on the Ritz, from the movie,
"Blue Skies."
LIFE December 31, 1945
13⅜ x 10⅝ inches

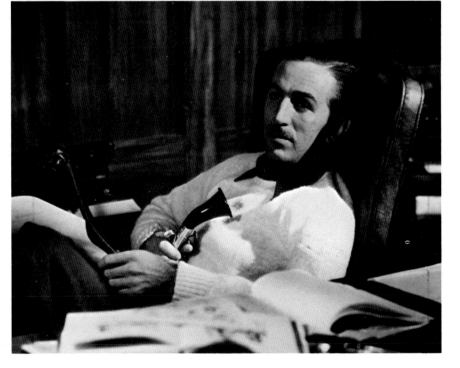

Gehr, Herbert/1943
Frank Sinatra, at 25, sings in a New York nightclub.
LIFE May 3, 1943
13¼ x 10⅝ inches

Stackpole, Peter/1941
Errol Flynn at the helm of his yacht, Sirocco.
13⅜ x 10¾ inches

Halsman, Philippe/1944
Humphrey Bogart.
13⅜ x 10⅝ inches

Connell, Will/1934
Walt Disney dictating an idea for a "Silly Symphony."
FORTUNE November 1934
7½ x 9½ inches   Signed and dated.

Capa, Robert/1946
Alfred Hitchcock directs cameraman to focus
on the key in Ingrid Bergman's hand in a
scene from "Notorious."
13⅛ x 10⅝ inches

Crane, Ralph/1944
Camera crane moves closer to photograph a
scene from "Bathing Beauty" starring Esther
Williams.
LIFE April 17, 1944
13⅝ x 10⅝ inches

Halsman, Philippe/1945
Lizabeth Scott in the motion picture, "You
Came Along."
13½ x 10⅝ inches

Bull, Clarence Sinclair/1934
Greta Garbo in the role of Sweden's 17th
century Queen Christina.
12¼ x 9 inches

Stackpole, Peter/1940
Vivien Leigh in a scene from "Gone With the
Wind."
LIFE May 20, 1940
13½ x 10⅝ inches

Gehr, Herbert/1941
Helena Rubinstein reads by the fluorescent
lighting which suffuses the head and foot of
her Lucite bed.
LIFE July 21, 1941
10½ x 13¼ inches

Halsman, Philippe/1943
Rita Hayworth, in "Cover Girl," poses for the
illustration of a pulp magazine story.
LIFE January 18, 1943
10⅞ x 13⅞ inches

Capa, Robert/1941
Ernest Hemingway and his youngest son,
Gregory, on a hunting trip near Sun Valley,
Idaho.
9⅛ x 13⅜ inches

Gehr, Herbert/1943
Toscanini watches himself in the movie
"Hymn of the Nations" which he and other
musicians made as a contribution to the U.S.
war effort.
TIME April 29, 1946
10¾ x 10⅜ inches

Stackpole, Peter/1944
Amusement arcade on 42nd Street
west of Broadway, New York City.
LIFE November 13, 1944
9⅜ x 13 inches

Coster, Gordon /1944
Four performers linger on the bare stage of
Chicago's Rialto Theater as its days as a
burlesque house come to an end.
LIFE September 18, 1944
10⅜ x 13¼ inches

Coster, Gordon/1944
The "mecca," substandard housing on
Chicago's south side.
LIFE July 17, 1944
10⅜ x 13¼ inches

Mieth, Hansel/1939
William Christopher Handy, composer of the
"St. Louis Blues."
LIFE July 7, 1941
13⅛ x 9¼ inches

Halsman, Philippe/1944
Yehudi Menuhin.
LIFE March 13, 1944
13⅝ x 11 inches

Halsman, Philippe/1944
Marian Anderson.
LIFE March 13, 1944
13⅝ x 10⅝ inches

Halsman, Philippe/1944
Wanda Landowska at the harpsichord.
TIME December 27, 1968
13¼ x 10⅝ inches

Da Miano, Andre/1937
Lionel Hampton.
10⅛ x 13¼ inches

Halsman, Philippe/1944
Artur Rubinstein.
12⅞ x 10½ inches

Bourke-White, Margaret/1937
Sonja Henie in the cafe scene from her movie,
"One in a Million."
10 x 13⅛ inches

Stackpole, Peter/1944
Marquee of the Astor motion picture theater,
Broadway, New York City.
13⅜ x 10½ inches

Abbott, Berenice/1936
Talman Street, between Jay and Bridge
Streets, Brooklyn, New York on May 22, 1936.
7¼ x 9⅜ inches

Abbott, Berenice
Numbers 4, 6, and 8 Fifth Ave., corner of 8th
St., New York City.
LIFE January 3, 1938
7½ x 9½ inches

Elisofon, Eliot/1942
Frank Lloyd Wright, master architect.
LIFE November 9, 1942
13¼ x 10¼ inches

Capa, Robert/1944
Pablo Picasso. From Capa's notes on this
assignment: "The only features of his mobile
face which remain the same are his eyes and
the smoke curling around his face from his
cigarette."
11⅞ x 10 inches

Coster, Gordon/1944
State Street, Chicago.
10¼ x 13¼ inches

Abbott, Berenice/1933
Exchange Place, one of the canyons of the
Wall Street financial district, New York City.
FORTUNE July 1939
9⅜ x 2 inches

Ljungdahl, Goesta P. G.
Albert Einstein.
LIFE April 11, 1938
12⅞ x 10⅛ inches

Karsh, Yousuf/1943
George Bernard Shaw.
12¾ x 10⅜ inches   Signed lower right.

Collins, John D./1940
Wendell Willkie, newly nominated as the
Republican presidential candidate, arriving in
his hometown of Elwood, Indiana to make his
acceptance speech.
LIFE September 2, 1940
10⅝ x 13¼ inches

106

Stackpole, Peter/1938
Fight between two cowboys at a bronco-
busting contest near Santa Fe, New Mexico.
LIFE October 24, 1938
10 x 13½ inches

Wide World/1937
Union and non-union workers clash at
Republic Steel's Corrigan-McKinney plant,
Cleveland.
LIFE December 26, 1960
10⅝ x 12¼ inches

Capa, Robert/1940
First fatality, election day, Mexico.
13¼ x 9⅞ inches

Beaton, Cecil/1940
Her Majesty Queen Elizabeth in the Blue
Drawing Room.
10¼ x 9¾ inches

Capa, Robert/1939
Duke and Duchess of Windsor at a boxing
match on the Côte d'Azur.
7 x 9½ inches

Skadding, George/1944
After his election to a fourth term, President
Roosevelt returns to Washington with his Vice
President, Henry A. Wallace, right, and his
Vice President-elect, Harry S. Truman, center.
LIFE November 20, 1944
10½ x 13⅜ inches

Davis, Myron/1945
Arthur B. Eisenhower and his grandson
Bradford welcome Arthur's brother, Dwight D.
Eisenhower, at his homecoming in Abilene,
Kansas at the end of World War II in Europe.
11 x 10½ inches

McAvoy, Thomas D./1938
After the formal portraits had been taken
at the Jackson Day Dinner and most
photographers had gone, leaving behind their
used flash bulbs, McAvoy caught President
Roosevelt in a relaxed mood.
LIFE January 24, 1938
6½ x 9½ inches

Wild, Hans/1945
Winston Churchill pauses at his easel in the
studio at Chartwell, his home in Kent.
LIFE January 7, 1946 Cover.
11⅞ x 9⅛ inches

Schall, Roger/1938
Eleven glasses and a knife and fork of gold
adorn the King's place at the luncheon given
for King George VI and Queen Elizabeth in
the Hall of Mirrors at Versailles.
LIFE August 15, 1938
8¼ x 7¾ inches

Bourke-White, Margaret/1940
Junction of Hamilton Terrace and Park Lane
during the London blackout.
7¼ x 9¾ inches

Beaton, Cecil/1940
Mrs. Lutwidge, mother of the pubkeeper's
wife, is a Victorian lady of good Yorkshire
family whose fortunes have dwindled.
LIFE November 18, 1940
10⅛ x 9¾ inches

Vandivert, William/1939
Bishop of Derby and his wife, Mrs. Rawlinson,
attend a garden party at Chatsworth House,
Devonshire.
9¾ x 7¾ inches

Eisenstaedt, Alfred/1934
In a flight over the Atlantic, Graf Zeppelin
crewmen climb out on the ship to repair storm
damage.
LIFE November 29, 1954
8⅞ x 12¾ inches   Signed on back.

Eisenstaedt, Alfred/1932
English couple at the ice bar at St. Moritz.
LIFE September 4, 1944
11¼ x 9 inches   Signed on back.

Stackpole, Peter/1941
Tourists take snapshots on a boat landing on
Lake Louise in the Canadian Rockies.
LIFE July 14, 1941
13¼ x 10¾ inches

Munkacsi, Martin/1939
Doris Duke Cromwell with her husband
James at their home in Honolulu.
LIFE March 20, 1939
11¼ x 8½ inches

Hardy, Rex Jr./1937
Woman waters her horse in the river between
Haiti and the Dominican Republic.
LIFE December 13, 1937
13¼ x 10¼ inches

Beaton, Cecil/1940
The Mayoress, Miss Edith Olivier, processes
to church, passing the entrance to Wilton
House, Wiltshire.
10⅛ x 9¾ inches

Sanders, Walter/1942
Young girl studies her image in the mirrored
section of a garden wall. Georgetown, in
Washington D.C.
10⅛ x 10⅛ inches

Smith, W. Eugene/1941
Joe Di Maggio.
13⅜ x 10⅛ inches

Mili, Gjon/1940
Study of Don McNeill's tennis form.
TIME August 4, 1941
12⅞ x 9⅞ inches

Mili, Gjon/1945
Carol Lynne's movements are recorded by
lights on her skates.
13¼ x 10⅜ inches

Capa, Robert/1939
Member of a hunting party in the Colorado
Mountains.
13½ x 9⅜ inches

Smith, W. Eugene/1941
Volleyball at Ohio Penitentiary at Columbus,
Ohio.
LIFE May 5, 1941
13¼ x 10½ inches

Salomon, Dr. Erich/1932
From the balcony outside his room at the
Lausanne Reparations Conference, Ramsay
MacDonald with his daughter Ishbel and his
private secretary Mr. Butler watch Premier
Herriot trying to avoid journalists who have
waylaid him in the lobby below.
FORTUNE September 1932
7 x 8⅛ inches

Salomon, Dr. Erich/1931
German Chancellor Heinrich Brüning argues
a point with French statesman Edouard
Herriot.
7¼ x 9½ inches

Salomon, Dr. Erich/1931
Benito Mussolini (left) and his Foreign
Minister Dino Grandi (right) entertain German
Chancellor Heinrich Brüning (facing camera)
and German Foreign Minister Julius Curtius
(back to camera) in Rome.
LIFE February 26, 1945
7⅛ x 9 inches

Salomon, Dr. Erich/1930
Reparation talks at 1:00 A.M. at the Hague. In
a weary group under the lamp are French
Premier Andre Tardieu, German Foreign
Minister Julius Curtius, and French Minister of
Finance Henri Cheron.
FORTUNE November 1931
7⅛ x 9⅜ inches

No Credit
Adolph Hitler makes his entrance at a mass
meeting at Buckeberg, 1934.
LIFE April 28, 1945
6⅛ x 9⅛ inches

Wide World
President Roosevelt reviews the U.S. fleet
from the bridge of the U.S.S. Houston. This
was one of his favorite photographs of
himself.
LIFE July 25, 1938
10⅝ x 13½ inches

Skadding, George/1944
General Charles De Gaulle arrives in
Washington for meetings with President
Roosevelt.
10½ x 13¼ inches

Bourke-White, Margaret/1941
Harry Hopkins with Joseph Stalin for
a series of meetings in the Kremlin.
LIFE September 8, 1941
13⅛ x 10⅛ inches

Beaton, Cecil/1941
Winston Churchill at the conference table in
the cabinet room of 10 Downing Street.
LIFE January 27, 1941
9⅛ x 9½ inches

Bourke-White, Margaret/1934
Dummy tanks of tin with wooden guns
conduct German maneuvers in 1934, one
year after Hitler came to power. The Treaty of
Versailles forbade Germany to rearm.
LIFE September 11, 1939
8 x 13¼ inches

Capa, Robert/1936
In Madrid, Loyalists joyfully watch
Government bombers attack a Rebel pursuit
plane.
LIFE December 28, 1936
6⅞ x 9¼ inches

Capa, Robert/1938
Ernest Hemingway in 1941 selected from
Capa's coverage of the Spanish Civil War
photographs he thought best illustrated
scenes in his new book, "For Whom the Bell
Tolls," which were then used in LIFE's review
of the book. Hemingway selected this
photograph to illustrate the moment in his
book when Robert Jordan detonated the hand
grenades to blow up the bridge.
LIFE January 6, 1941
7 x 9⅜ inches

Kessel, Dmitri/1945
Daughter of one of the 1,000 citizens
slaughtered by the Germans in the Greek
town of Distomo mourns her mother months
after the massacre.
LIFE November 27, 1944
9⅞ x 10¾ inches   Signed on back.

Pictures, Inc./1936
Maria Garcia, leader of the Loyalist women's
militia, with some of her troops in Barcelona.
LIFE November 23, 1936
10 x 12 inches

Vishniac, Roman
From an essay on the misery and poverty of
life in the Polish ghetto.
9⅞ x 8 inches

Interphoto/1939
Through a pass in the Pyrenees, Spanish
refugees drag their belongings down into a
valley of France.
LIFE February 20, 1939
6⅜ x 9 inches

International News Photo/1942
Malayan mother grief-stricken at the death of
her child during a Japanese attack on
Singapore.
LIFE March 23, 1942
10¼ x 13⅜ inches

Daly, Kelso/1941
Pearl Harbor inhabitant watches bombing by
Japanese planes.
LIFE January 5, 1942
11 x 13⅞ inches

Dorsey, Paul/1938
Japanese soldiers wave good-bye to their
friends in a Toyko railroad station as they
leave to fight in the war against China.
LIFE July 10, 1939
10½ x 13½ inches

Eisenstaedt, Alfred/1942
Missouri draft board studies a young farmer.
LIFE November 9, 1942
14¼ x 10⅜ inches   Signed on back.

Strock, George/1940
At Fort Dix, New Jersey, a draftee gets
simultaneous smallpox and typhoid injections
from medical officers in the first peacetime
draft, November 1940.
LIFE December 9, 1940
10¼ x 13¼ inches

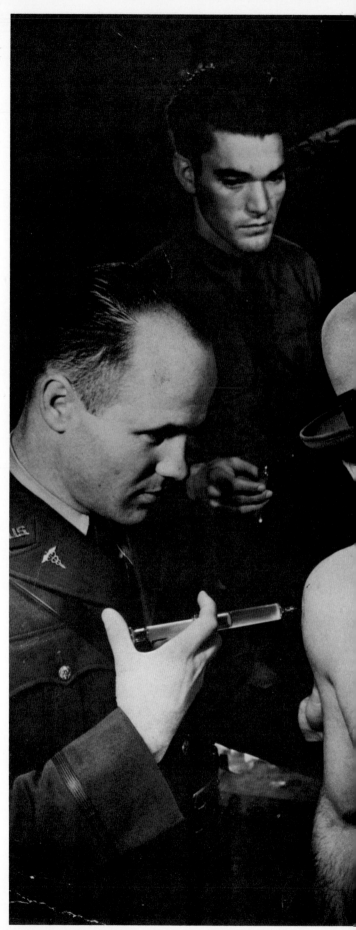

Mydans, Carl/1944
Young Japanese Nisei at Tule Lake
Internment Camp, California, whiles away his
time playing a guitar.
LIFE March 20, 1944
13 x 8⅞ inches   Signed on back.

Sanders, Walter/1943
Betty Grable models a coat decorated with
Army corps and rank insignia.
LIFE June 7, 1943
13¼ x 10¼ inches

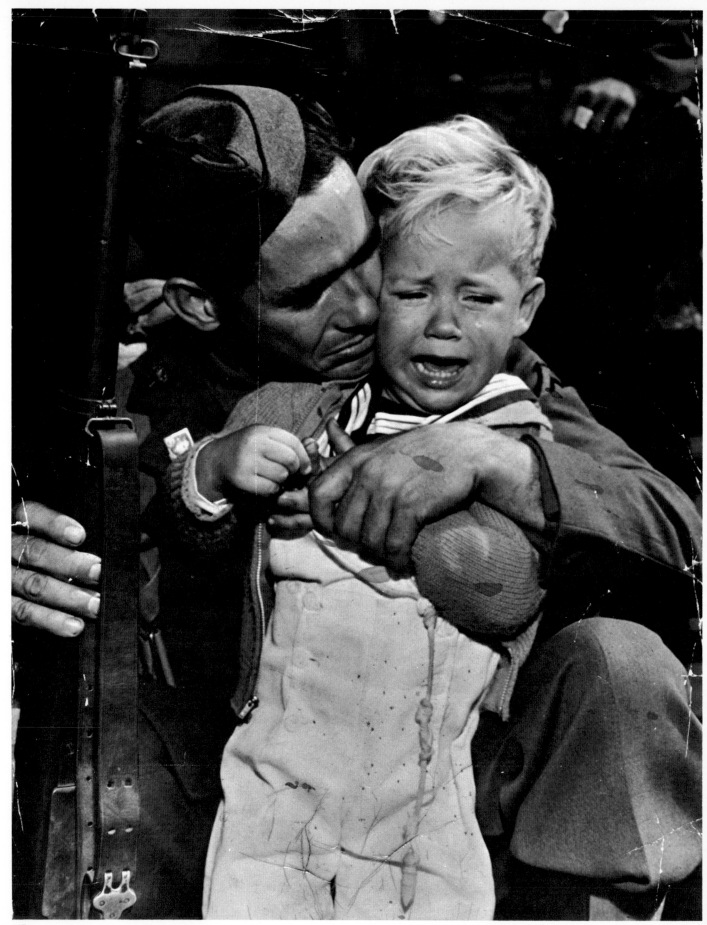

147

Eisenstaedt, Alfred/1944
Sailor saying good-bye at Pennsylvania
Station.
LIFE February 14, 1944
13¼ x 10¼ inches   Signed on back.

**Jakobsen, Robert, Los Angeles
Times**/1940
Private John Winbury of the California
National Guard says good-bye to his son
before he leaves for Hawaii.
LIFE November 25, 1940
13⅝ x 10⅝ inches

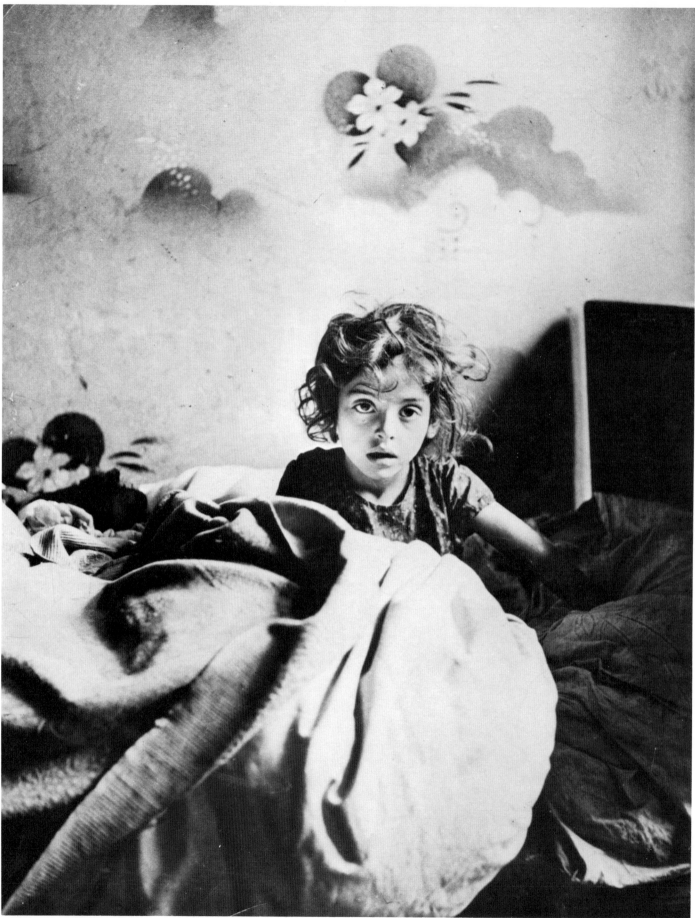

149

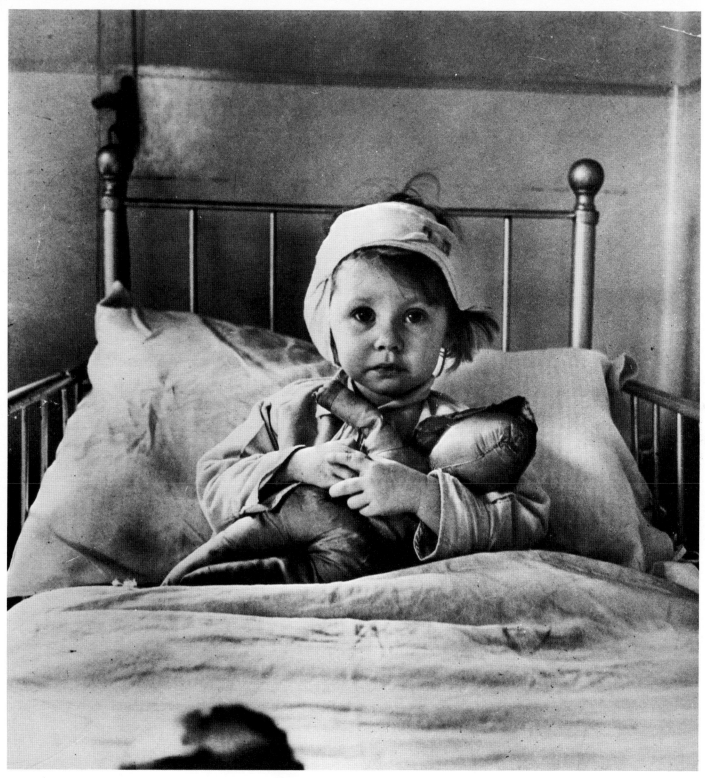

Vishniac, Roman
Girl, weak from hunger, lives in bed to
conserve her strength. The flowers on the wall
of their house in the Polish ghetto were
painted by her father.
LIFE May 8, 1944
10 x 8 inches

Beaton, Cecil/1940
Three-year-old child recovering from a head
injury suffered in German air blitz on her North
England village.
LIFE September 23, 1940 Cover
11¼ x 10⅝ inches

Vishniac, Roman
Children of the Polish ghetto enjoy three
weeks in the country before returning to their
home in a cellar.
8 x 9⅞ inches

Beaton, Cecil/1940
English children, war evacuees, troop across
the lawn of the country estate where they are
sheltered.
10¼ x 9¾ inches

Capa, Robert/1944
Normandy Invasion on D-Day, June 6, 1944.
Capa's notes read, "First troops hit the
beachhead and lie down under heavy artillery
and machine gun fire from the pillboxes…
Note landing craft in background."
LIFE June 19, 1944
8⅞ x 13⅜ inches

Capa, Robert/1944
Troops advancing on the Normandy beach
after leaving the landing craft.
LIFE June 19, 1944
8⅞ x 13⅜ inches

Yugoslva Army/1943
Death of a young soldier during the epic
Partisan march through the Green Mountain
when Tito and four divisions eventually broke
through the German army which completely
encircled them.
9¼ x 7 inches

Bourke-White, Margaret/1940
Cameron Highlanders and Indian Troops
drilling in front of the Great Pyramid near
Cairo.
LIFE July 29, 1940
10⅛ x 13½ inches

Bourke-White, Margaret/1944
Supporting fire for a nighttime infantry probe
of German positions on the Italian front in the
spring of 1944.
LIFE April 16, 1945
13¼ x 9⅝ inches

British Official Photograph/1943
Pillars of smoke billow more than three miles
into the air over Dusseldorf after the RAF's
raid on June 11-12, 1943. Wavy light trails are
caused by burning incendiaries.
LIFE September 27, 1943
9⅜ x 11⅜ inches

Silk, George/1945
Marlene Dietrich entertains American troops
in Germany.
LIFE March 5, 1945
11 x 10½ inches   Signed on back.

**Official Navy Photo: Captain Edward
Steichen's Division**/1943
Setting-up exercises on a converted aircraft
carrier in the African convoy.
10⅜ x 10½ inches

Bourke-White, Margaret/1944
GIs use the portico of a 15th century Italian monastery for their early morning washing and shaving.
9¾ x 13½ inches

International News Photos/1940
Great dome of St. Paul's Cathedral
surrounded by the burning city of London
during a major incendiary bomb attack in
December of 1940. The Cathedral was saved.
LIFE January 27, 1941
7⅜ x 9⅜ inches

Wild, Hans/1941
Bell towers of St. Paul's Cathedral are seen
through smouldering ruins after a German air
raid on London.
LIFE January 27, 1941
12 x 10 inches

Bourke-White, Margaret/1945
From notes by Bourke-White accompanying
her film: "Mainz…showing center of town with
ruined churches and roofless buildings."
10⅝ x 13½ inches

London Daily Mirror/1940
Mrs. Bidecant of London's East End serves
dinner to a family whose home, seen through
the window, was demolished in an air raid.
LIFE October 7, 1940
11½ x 8 inches

Beaton, Cecil/1941
Prime Minister Churchill's walking sticks. The
one on the left is fitted with a flashlight for
use in the blackout. The portrait below the
barometer is of Sir George Downing, who built
No. 10 Downing Street.
LIFE January 27, 1941
10⅛ x 9⅞ inches

Rodger, George/1945
Small boy walks past corpses at Belsen
extermination camp. Rodger captioned his
film with a description of what he and the
Allied soldiers found at the camp: "Dead lying
by the side of one of the roads in the camp.
They die like this in thousands. There are
piles of them in among the pine trees. The SS
Guards gave them neither food nor water.
When they became so weak they could no
longer walk they just lay down wherever they
were."
LIFE May 7, 1945
10⅝ x 10⅜ inches

Vandivert, William/1945
Some of the political prisoners who vainly
tried to escape when the barn in which they
were housed was set on fire by the Nazis as
the American forces drew closer.
LIFE May 7, 1945
10⅝ x 10⅝ inches

Bourke-White, Margaret/1945
Victims of the Buchenwald concentration camp. Bourke-White wrote to LIFE's editors the day she took this and the following photograph: "The sights I have just seen are so unbelievable that I don't think I'll believe them myself until I've seen the photographs ….The important thing about today was not just the camp itself but the fact that the German civilians WERE BEING FORCED TO LOOK AT WHAT THEIR PARTY LEADERS HAD DONE. [*Capitalization is Bourke-White's*] General Patton ordered *1,000* people to come out this afternoon to see the victims …I managed to arrive just as large parties of these Germans were being conducted into the camp….The most incredible sight of all was in the court just outside the incinerator plant. A central truck was piled high with naked bodies of the recent dead. A pile of newly dead bodies lay nearby."
10⅞ x 10¾ inches

Bourke-White, Margaret/1945
German civilians at Buchenwald
concentration camp. Bourke-White's captions
continue: "The German civilians were next led
past the pile of bodies into the open court and
stood facing the central tumbrel of corpses…
Many women put handkerchiefs over their
eyes. They could not bear to look."
10⅝ x 10⅝ inches

Tames, George/1945
Grieving woman waves farewell as President
Roosevelt's funeral procession moves down
Pennsylvania Avenue.
TIME April 23, 1945
7⅝ x 7⅝ inches

Morse, Ralph/1945
Parisians rejoice around the Arc de Triomphe,
illuminated and hung with flags after the
German garrison surrendered.
10⅝ x 10⅝ inches

Bourke-White, Margaret/1945
Mayor of Leipzig and his wife and daughter
commit suicide by taking poison when the
Americans enter the city.
LIFE May 14, 1945
Each 4½ x 6¼ inches

Capa, Robert/1945
From Capa's notes accompanying this
photograph: "…a member of the machine gun
platoon covering infantry advance takes over
gun on open balcony where American
sergeant has just been killed by German
sniper."
LIFE May 14, 1945
9⅛ x 13½ inches

Scherschel, Frank/1944
Crowd which had gathered to participate
in ceremonies marking the liberation of
Paris crouches in panic under fire from
collaborationist snipers.
LIFE November 5, 1945
12 x 10¾ inches

McCombe, Leonard/1945
Homeless German refugees huddle in a
Berlin municipal building seeking shelter.
LIFE October 15, 1945
12⅛ x 13½ inches

Capa, Robert/1944
German snipers who fired on crowd
celebrating liberation of Paris had to be
protected from infuriated citizens when they
were captured.
LIFE September 11, 1944
13½ x 10½ inches

Interphoto/1940
Belgian girl, convicted of treason, being led
to her execution by a firing squad.
LIFE June 17, 1940
7 x 6¼ inches

Mydans, Carl/1944
Execution of French traitors. From Mydans'
captions: "Before the blank wall of a factory in
Grenoble six French youths found guilty of
treason to France were executed by a rifle
squad. Officers went quickly to them and fired
a coup de grace into each."
LIFE October 2, 1944
6¼ x 9⅜ inches   Signed on back.

Scherman, David/1945
Fernand De Brinon, a major collaborationist,
testifies at Marshall Petain's trial for treason
that Petain had been just a tool and did not
know what was going on.
TIME April 28, 1947
7½ x 7⅝ inches

Rodger, George/1944
At Breendonk, a notorious prison run by the
Nazis in occupied Antwerp, a Flemish SS
Guard becomes a prisoner himself after the
overthrow of the German forces.
4¾ x 4¾ inches

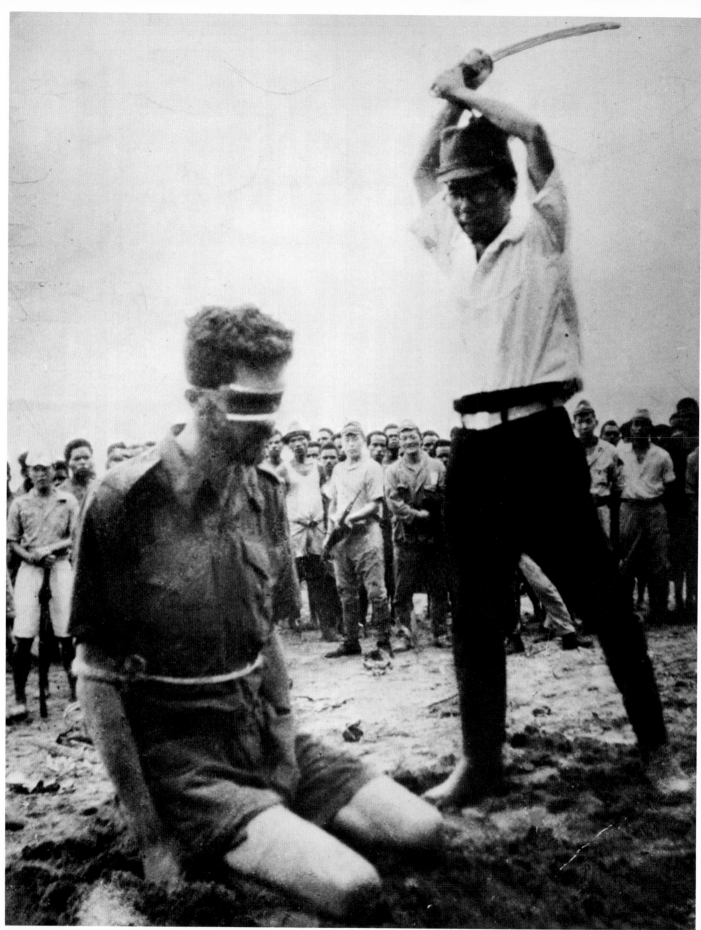

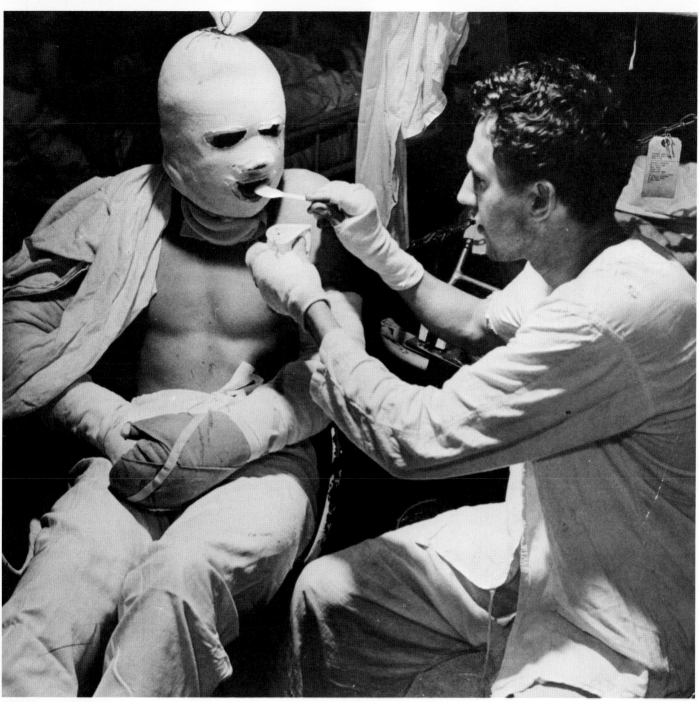

Official U.S. Navy Photo.
Sailor, severely burned in a Pacific battle, is
fed a little ice cream.
LIFE August 20, 1945
7⅜ x 7⅞ inches

No Credit.
Japanese officer about to behead a captured
Australian pilot.
LIFE May 14, 1945
7⅞ x 6 inches

Strock, George/1943
This photograph of the bodies of three
American soldiers ambushed on Buna Beach,
New Guinea was one of the first to show U.S.
personnel killed in World War II combat.
LIFE September 20, 1943
13⅜ x 10⅜ inches

Smith, W. Eugene/1944
In a Philippine church serving as a hospital, a
U.S. Army nurse checks on her patient.
LIFE December 25, 1944
10⅞ x 10⅝ inches

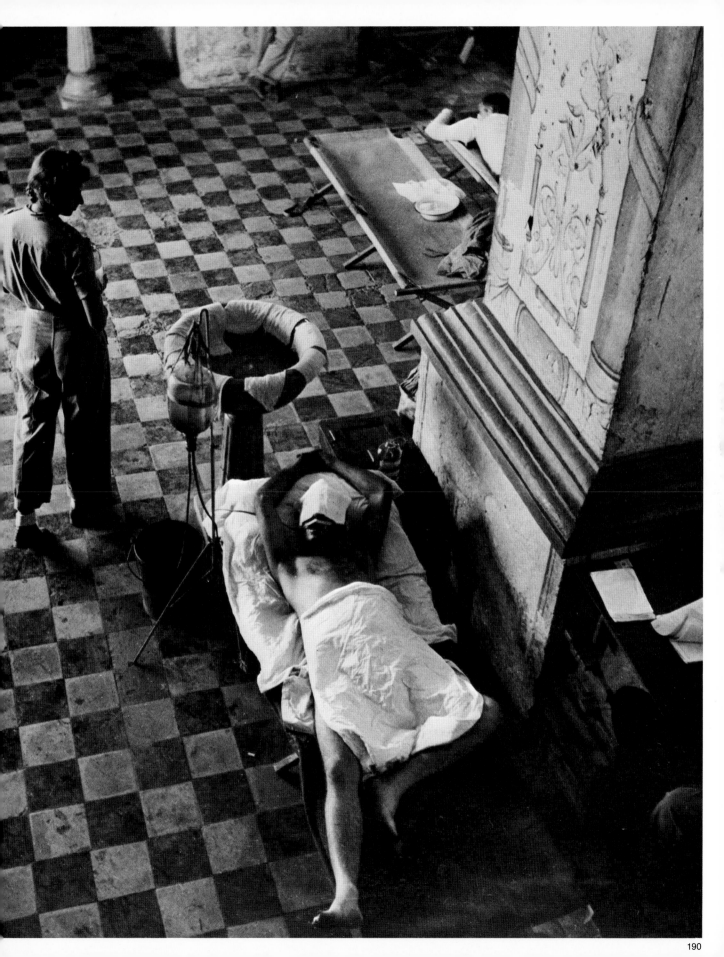

Smith, W. Eugene/1944
Men wounded during the landing on Guam
are evacuated by amphibious truck.
10¾ x 10⅝ inches

Smith, W. Eugene/1945
Clearing Japanese out of the caves on
Saipan. Smith's caption accompanying this
photograph reads: "The first live person that
we found was a 'living-dead' tiny infant that
had somehow become lodged with face
straight down into the dirt and head almost
concealed by being wedged under the edge
of a rock...We had heard the tiny muffled cry
and then had seen the bony body writhing
with its head as pivot."
LIFE November 5, 1945
13¾ x 11¼ inches

Smith, W. Eugene/1945
Marines blow up a cave connected to a
Japanese blockhouse on Iwo Jima.
LIFE April 9, 1945 Cover.
9⅜ x 13¼ inches

Smith, W. Eugene/1945
Smith wrote of his photograph of a man
wounded in the battle for Okinawa: "…a
soldier hit in the head is treated by the medic
and put on a litter to be carried to the rear.
Conscious, he was in great pain but could
not be given morphine because of his
head wound."
6½ x 9½ inches

Smith, W. Eugene/1944
Grave of one of the few unknown Marine dead
of World War II. In the cemetery of the 4th
Division Marines on Saipan.
LIFE August 28, 1944
10⅜ x 10⅝ inches

Mydans, Carl, via/1945
Remains of the city of Nagasaki after an
atomic bomb had been dropped.
August 9, 1945.
7¼ x 5¼ inches

Silk, George/1945
Before a household shrine, all that remains of
her home, a Japanese woman prays for her
husband killed in the firebombing of Tokyo.
LIFE December 3, 1945
13⅜ x 10½ inches   Signed on back.

Morse, Ralph/1943
Head of a Japanese tankman is displayed by
U.S. troops on a burned-out Japanese tank,
Guadalcanal in the Solomon Islands.
LIFE February 1, 1943
13⅞ x 10¼ inches

McAvoy, Thomas D./1945
Father returning home after nearly four years
in a Japanese prison camp is greeted by his
son.
LIFE October 8, 1945
13⅜ x 10⅝ inches

Morse, Ralph/1945
French prisoner of war, returning home after
five years, is greeted by his wife.
13½ x 10¾ inches

Eisenstaedt, Alfred/1942
Students erupt from class in a Garden City,
Long Island grade school.
10⅝ x 13¼ inches   Signed on back.

Smith, W. Eugene/1941
British sailor on leave in the U.S. registers
unabashed interest in American girls.
LIFE June 16, 1941
13¼ x 10½

Stackpole, Peter/1937
LIFE goes to a party in Philadelphia.
LIFE March 8, 1937
10 x 11¼ inches

Sanders, Walter/1941
Students at a Kansas college decide to hold a
blanket party.
LIFE May 26, 1941
10¾ x 10⅛

Index

ABBOTT, BERENICE 99, 100, 102
ADAMS, ANSEL 14, 50
BEATON, CECIL 44, 67, 109, 117, 123, 134, 150, 152, 168
BOURKE-WHITE, MARGARET 1, 21, 24, 28, 31, 33, 35, 36, 68, 97, 116, 133, 135, 156, 157, 162, 165, 171, 172, 175, 176
BRISTOL, HORACE 8, 11, 12
BRODSKY, MICHEL 48
BULL, CLARENCE SINCLAIR 82
CAPA, ROBERT 79, 85, 103, 108, 110, 127, 136, 153, 154, 177, 180
COLLINS, JOHN 105
CONNELL, WILL 78
COOKE, JERRY 75
COSTER, GORDON 16, 91, 92, 101
CRANE, RALPH 80
DA MIANO, ANDRE 96
DALY, KELSO 141
DAVIS, MYRON 112
DORSEY, PAUL 142
EDGERTON, HAROLD 39
EISENSTAEDT, ALFRED 3, 6, 7, 22, 54, 69, 70, 89, 119, 121, 143, 148, 202
ELISOFON, ELIOT 103
EVANS, WALKER 40
FEININGER, ANDREAS 29
GEHR, HERBERT 19, 56, 77, 83, 86
GORO, FRITZ 46
HALSMAN, PHILIPPE 78, 81, 84, 93, 94, 95, 96
HARDY, REX 122
HARRIS, MARTIN 66
JACKSON, RAY LEE 52
JAKOBSEN, ROBERT 147
KARSH, YOUSUF 104
KESSEL, DMITRI 138
KITROSSER, I. 55
KORLING, TORKEL 57, 58
LANDRY, BOB 76

LEEN, NINA 43
LJUNGDAHL, GOESTA 104
LOFMAN, JACOB 26
McAVOY, THOMAS 113, 199
McCOMBE, LEONARD 179
MANZON 47
MIETH, HANSEL 93
MILI, GJON 64, 125, 126
MORSE, RALPH 174, 198, 200
MUNKACSI, MARTIN 42, 51, 59, 65, 74, 122
MYDANS, CARL 9, 23, 145, 182, 185, 196
O'REILLY, GRAY 72
PRINCE, ERNEY 71
RODGER, GEORGE 169, 184
ROTHSTEIN, ARTHUR 5
SALOMON, ERICH 129, 130
SANDERS, WALTER 124, 146, 204
SARRA, VALENTINO 38
SCHALL, ROGER 115
SCHERMAN, DAVID 53, 183
SCHERSCHEL, FRANK 178
SHEELER, CHARLES 30
SILK, GEORGE 159, 197
SKADDING, GEORGE 111, 133
SMITH, W. EUGENE 20, 62, 125, 128, 190, 191, 192, 193, 194, 195, 201
STACKPOLE, PETER 25, 49, 60, 78, 82, 87, 98, 107, 122, 203
STERN, PHIL 4
STROCK, GEORGE 144, 189
TAMES, GEORGE 173
VANDIVERT, WILLIAM 18, 118, 170
VAN DYKE, WILLARD 41
VISHNIAC, ROMAN 139, 149, 151
WESTON, EDWARD 45
WILD, HANS 114, 164
WILDING, DOROTHY 73